IN 1976, JANE FRIEDMAN, A FREELANCE NEW YORK PUBLICIST AND MANAGER OF SUCH ARTISTS AS PATTI SMITH, TOM VERLAINE AND JOHN CALE, ASKED IF I WOULD PHOTOGRAPH THESE 'THREE GREAT-LOOKING ENGLISH BLOND ROCK AND ROLLERS' (THAT'S THE WAY WE AMERICAN GIRLS TALK TO EACH OTHER, YA KNOW!). I TRUSTED JANE'S TASTE AND WENT TO THE IROQUOIS HOTEL TO DO THE PHOTOGRAPHS. I ARRIVED A FEW MINUTES EARLY AND WAITED TO GO TO THE ROOM AT THE ALLOTTED TIME, BUT BEFORE I COULD, THE ELEVATOR DOOR OPENED AND OUT POPPED THE POLICE. ANDY LOOKED SO VERY SMALL NEXT TO STEWART WHO LOOKED SO VERY TALL NEXT TO ANDY . . . AND THEN THERE WAS STING WITH THESE ROUND GLASSES AND SPIKED HAIR. HE WAS READING SOMETHING EXISTENTIAL. I THOUGHT, HOW COULD JANE HAVE LIED TO ME? (KIDDING . . . ONLY KIDDING.)

□ I WANT TO THANK HER NOW AS WELL AS MILES COPELAND, MANAGER OF THE POLICE, THROUGH WHOM IT WAS POSSIBLE TO GET ON THE 'INSIDE'. TO BE LET INTO THE LIVES OF OTHER PEOPLE, ESPECIALLY WHEN YOU ARE CARRYING A CAMERA, IS AN EXPERIENCE WHICH I BELIEVE CAN ENRICH ONE'S LIFE.

□ IN SHARING THESE 'FLASHES OF INSIGHT' WITH YOU, I HAVE CHOSEN TO USE APHORISMS AS CAPTIONS SINCE THEY ARE LIKE MY PHOTO-GRAPHS – OBSERVATIONS, DISCOVERIES . . . DETACHED GLIMPSES. APHORISMS ARE UNIVERSAL YET NOT IMPERSONAL. THEY ARE SUBVERSIVE AND MUST BE ABLE TO STAND ON THEIR OWN. APHORISMS ARE LIKE STING, STEWART AND ANDY, AN UNSETTLING PARADOX.

LYNN GOLDSMITH

THE
POLICE

ASK ME NO QUESTIONS, AND I'LL TELL YOU NO FIBS □
OLIVER GOLDSMITH: *SHE STOOPS TO CONQUER*, III, 1

ST. MARTIN'S PRESS
NEW YORK

FIRST PUBLISHED IN 1983 IN GREAT BRITAIN BY VERMILION BOOKS.

FIRST U.S. EDITION

10 9 8 7 6 5 4 3 2 1

ISBN 0-312-61995-2

TO ANDY CAVALIERE
BECAUSE HE OPENED MY EYES WITH HIS HEART

FLOAT LIKE A BUTTERFLY, STING LIKE A BEE □ BUNDINI

AN APPLE A DAY KEEPS THE DOCTOR AWAY □
ANONYMOUS

MAN SHALL NOT LIVE BY BREAD ALONE □ *NEW TESTAMENT, MATTHEW, IV, 4*

IT TAKES A SOUND REALIST TO MAKE A CONVINCING
SYMBOLIST □ D. J. ENRIGHT: *THE APOTHECARY'S SHOP*

SOMEBODY'S BORING ME . . . I THINK IT'S ME □ DYLAN
THOMAS

SOME PEOPLE ARE MOULDED BY THEIR ADMIRATIONS,
OTHERS BY THEIR HOSTILITIES ☐ ELIZABETH BOWEN:
THE DEATH OF THE HEART

A MAN'S MOST OPEN ACTIONS HAVE A SECRET SIDE TO
THEM □ JOSEPH CONRAD: *UNDER WESTERN EYES*

IT TAKES A NONENTITY TO THINK OF EVERYTHING □
HONORÉ DE BALZAC: *PIERRE GRASSOU*

UNLESS ONE IS A GENIUS, IT IS BEST TO AIM AT BEING
INTELLIGIBLE □ ANTHONY HOPE: *THE DOLLY
DIALOGUES*

DON'T FOLLOW LEADERS, WATCH THE PARKIN' METERS
☐ BOB DYLAN

BEES ARE NOT AS BUSY AS WE THINK THEY ARE. THEY
JUST CAN'T BUZZ ANY SLOWER □ KIN HUBBARD: *ABE
MARTIN'S SAYINGS*

THE REBEL ANGELS FLY IN RANKS □ HENRI PETIT:
LES JUSTES SOLITUDES

MAN CONSIDERS THE ACTIONS, BUT GOD WEIGHS THE
INTENTIONS □ THOMAS A KEMPIS: *THE IMITATION
OF CHRIST*

CAN WE IMAGINE IT POSSIBLE, THAT WHILE HUMAN
NATURE REMAINS THE SAME, MEN WILL EVER BECOME
ENTIRELY INDIFFERENT TO THEIR POWER, RICHES,
BEAUTY OR PERSONAL MERIT, AND THAT THEIR PRIDE
AND VANITY WILL NOT BE AFFECTED BY THESE
ADVANTAGES? □ HUME: *A TREATISE OF HUMAN
NATURE*

THE BEST PLACE TO SEEK GOD IS IN A GARDEN. YOU
CAN DIG FOR HIM THERE □ GEORGE BERNARD SHAW:
ADVENTURES OF THE BLACK GIRL

FAITH IS UNDER THE LEFT NIPPLE □ MARTIN LUTHER

THOUGHTS ARE THE SHADOWS OF OUR FEELINGS –
ALWAYS DARKER, EMPTIER AND SIMPLER □ NIETZSCHE:
THE GAY SCIENCE

ONE CAN BE BORED UNTIL BOREDOM BECOMES A
MYSTICAL EXPERIENCE □ LOGAN PEARSALL SMITH:
AFTERTHOUGHTS

THOSE WHO HAVE SOME MEANS THINK THAT THE
MOST IMPORTANT THING IN THE WORLD IS LOVE. THE
POOR KNOW THAT IT IS MONEY □ GERALD BRENAN:
THOUGHTS IN A DRY SEASON

IN A MAN'S WORK THERE IS A GRAVITY WHICH HE
HIMSELF DOES NOT POSSESS □ DELACROIX: *JOURNAL*

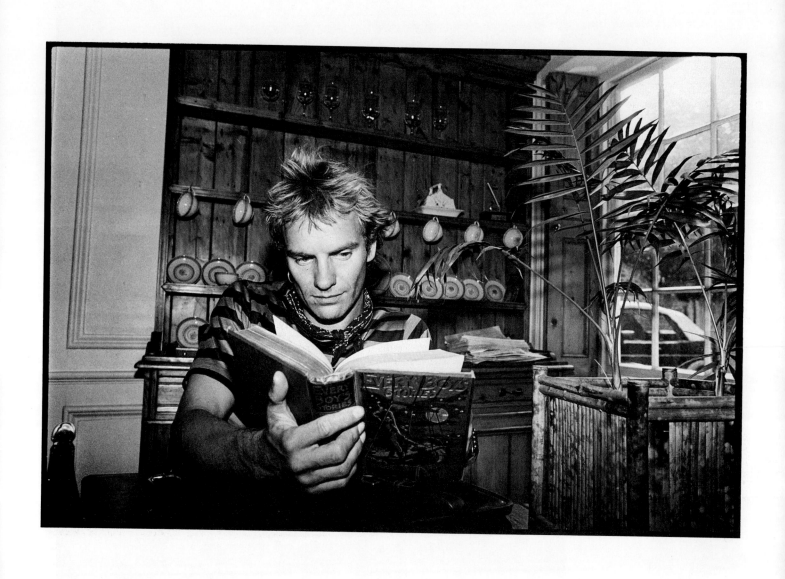

ONE'S REAL LIFE IS SO OFTEN THE LIFE THAT ONE DOES
NOT LEAD □ OSCAR WILDE: *L'ENVOI TO 'ROSE-LEAF*
AND APPLE-LEAF'

IF YOU WANT TO GET RICH, YOU SON OF A BITCH, I'LL
TELL YOU WHAT TO DO: NEVER SIT DOWN WITH A TEAR
OR A FROWN AND PADDLE YOUR OWN CANOE □
ANONYMOUS

SOMEWHERE AT THE HEART OF THE UNIVERSE SOUNDS
THE TRUE MYSTIC NOTE: ME □ PETER PORTER:
THE LAST OF ENGLAND

THE VOICE IS A SECOND FACE □ GERARD BAUER:
CARNETS

MEN SOMETIMES FEEL INJURED BY PRAISE BECAUSE IT
ASSIGNS A LIMIT TO THEIR MERIT □ VAUVENARGUES:
REFLECTIONS AND MAXIMS

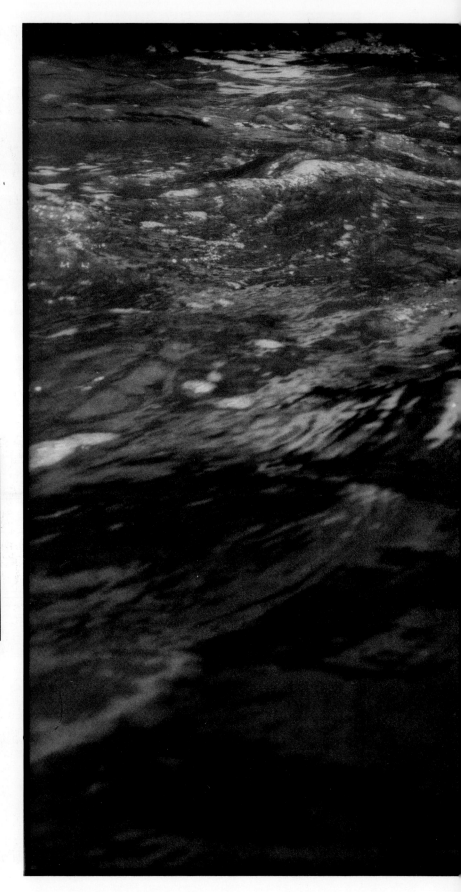

WHAT IS PECULIAR IN THE LIFE OF A MAN CONSISTS
NOT IN HIS OBEDIENCE, BUT IN HIS OPPOSITION TO
HIS INSTINCTS. IN ONE DIRECTION OR ANOTHER HE
STRIVES TO LIVE A SUPERNATURAL LIFE ☐ THOREAU:
JOURNAL

BEFORE DOING SOMEONE A FAVOUR, MAKE SURE
THAT HE ISN'T A MADMAN □ EUGENE LABICHE:
LE VOYAGE DE M. PERRICHON

THE ART OF BEING WISE IS THE ART OF KNOWING
WHAT TO OVERLOOK □ WILLIAM JAMES: *PRINCIPLES
OF PSYCHOLOGY*

SOMEBODY'S BORING ME . . . I THINK IT'S ME □
DYLAN THOMAS

INVENTION IS THE MOTHER OF NECESSITY □
THORSTEIN VERBLEN

SOMETIMES IN LIFE, SITUATIONS DEVELOP THAT ONLY
THE HALF-CRAZY CAN GET OUT OF □
LA ROCHEFOUCAULD: *MAXIMS*

IN THE HUMAN HEART NEW PASSIONS ARE FOR EVER
BEING BORN; THE OVER-THROW ALMOST ALWAYS
MEANS THE RISE OF ANOTHER □ LA ROCHEFOUCAULD:
MAXIMS

PATIENCE IS THE PANACEA; BUT WHERE DOES IT GROW,
OR WHO CAN SWALLOW IT? □ WILLIAM SHENSTONE:
ESSAYS ON MEN AND MANNERS

A JEALOUS MAN ALWAYS FINDS MORE THAN HE IS
LOOKING FOR □ MADELEINE DE SCUDÉRY:
DE LA JALOUSIE

EVERY MAN HAS A MOB SELF AND AN INDIVIDUAL SELF,
IN VARYING PROPORTIONS □ D. H. LAWRENCE:
PORNOGRAPHY AND OBSCENITY

EVERYTHING IS WORTHY OF NOTICE, FOR EVERYTHING
CAN BE INTERPRETED □ HERMANN HESSE: *THE GLASS
BEAD GAME*

THERE ARE NO SECRETS EXCEPT THE SECRETS THAT KEEP
THEMSELVES □ GEORGE BERNARD SHAW:
BACK TO METHUSELAH

IF I OWNED TEXAS AND HELL, I WOULD RENT OUT TEXAS
AND LIVE IN HELL ☐ GENERAL PHILIP H. SHERIDAN

WHAT IS HECUBA TO HIM, OR HE TO HECUBA? □
SHAKESPEARE: *HAMLET*, II, 2

EVERYTHING COMES TO THOSE WHO WAIT ☐ MILTON:
SONNET: 'ON HIS BLINDNESS'

UP TO A CERTAIN POINT EVERY MAN IS WHAT HE
THINKS HE IS □ F. H. BRADY: *APHORISMS*

HAIN'T WE GOT ALL THE FOOLS IN TOWN ON OUR
SIDE? AND HAIN'T THAT A BIG ENOUGH MAJORITY IN
ANY TOWN? ☐ MARK TWAIN: *HUCKLEBERRY FINN*

THERE IS A CERTAIN DISTANCE AT WHICH EACH
PERSON WE KNOW IS NATURALLY PLACED FROM US. IT
VARIES WITH EACH, AND WE MUST NOT ATTEMPT TO
ALTER IT. WE MAY CLASP HIM WHO IS CLOSE, AND WE
ARE NOT TO PULL CLOSER HIM WHO IS MORE REMOTE
□ MARK RUTHERFORD: *MORE PAGES FROM A JOURNAL*

IN HEAVEN AN ANGEL IS NOBODY IN PARTICULAR □
GEORGE BERNARD SHAW: 'MAXIMS FOR
REVOLUTIONISTS', *MAN AND SUPERMAN*

WE LIVE BEYOND ANY TALE WE HAPPEN TO ENACT □
V. S. PRITCHETT: *THE MYTH MAKERS*

INDIVIDUALITY SEEMS TO BE NATURE'S WHOLE AIM
AND SHE CARES NOTHING FOR THE INDIVIDUAL □
GOETHE: *MAXIMS AND REFLECTIONS*

WHILE WE STUDY WITH ATTENTION THE VANITY OF HUMAN LIFE, AND
TURN ALL OUR THOUGHTS TOWARDS THE EMPTY AND TRANSITORY
NATURE OF RICHES AND HONOURS, WE ARE, PERHAPS, ALL THE WHILE
FLATTERING OUR NATURAL INDOLENCE □ HUME: *PHILOSOPHICAL
ESSAYS CONCERNING HUMAN UNDERSTANDING*

WHAT IS VANITY, BUT THE LONGING TO SURVIVE? □
MIGUEL DE UNAMUNO: *THE TRAGIC SENSE OF LIFE*

AN ARTIST IS A PERSON WHO HAS INVENTED AN ARTIST
□ HAROLD ROSENBERG: *DISCOVERING THE PRESENT*

HOW DREARY TO BE SOMEBODY!
HOW PUBLIC, LIKE A FROG
TO TELL YOUR NAME THE LIVELONG DAY
TO AN ADMIRING BOG! □
EMILY DICKINSON: *POEMS I*

CAESAR WAS TOO OLD, IT SEEMS TO ME, TO GO OFF
AND AMUSE HIMSELF CONQUERING THE WORLD.
SUCH A PASTIME WAS ALL RIGHT FOR AUGUSTUS AND
ALEXANDER; THEY WERE YOUNG MEN, NOT EASILY
HELD IN CHECK, BUT CAESAR OUGHT TO HAVE BEEN
MORE MATURE □ PASCAL: *PENSÉES*

BECOMING ACCUSTOMED TO CERTAIN SOUNDS HAS
A PROFOUND EFFECT ON CHARACTER; SOON ONE
ACQUIRES THE WORDS AND PHRASES AND EVENTUALLY
ALSO THE IDEAS THAT GO WITH THESE SOUNDS □
NIETZSCHE: *THE GAY SCIENCE*

HERE'S A SIGH TO THOSE WHO LOVE ME,
AND A SMILE TO THOSE WHO HATE;
AND, WHATEVER SKY'S ABOVE ME,
HERE'S A HEART FOR ANY FATE. □
BYRON: *TO THOMAS MOORE*

NO MAN IS A HERO TO HIS VALET □ MADAME
CORNUEL: *LETTRES*

THEY ALSO SERVE WHO ONLY STAND AND WAIT □
MILTON: *SONNET: ON HIS BLINDNESS*

GREAT MEN ARE BUT LIFE-SIZED. MOST OF THEM,
INDEED, ARE RATHER SHORT □ MAX BEERBOHM:
AND EVEN NOW

WHEN SMASHING MONUMENTS, SAVE THE PEDESTALS
– THEY ALWAYS COME IN HANDY □ STANISLAW LEM:
UNKEMPT THOUGHTS

I CAN RESIST EVERYTHING EXCEPT TEMPTATION ☐
OSCAR WILDE: *LADY WINDERMERE'S FAN*

WHEN I GIVE A HUNDRED-FRANC BILL, I GIVE THE
DIRTIEST ONE □ JULES RENARD: *JOURNAL*

WHEN DEALING WITH THE INSANE, THE BEST METHOD
IS TO PRETEND TO BE SANE □ HERMANN HESSE:
PROSA AND FEUILLETONS

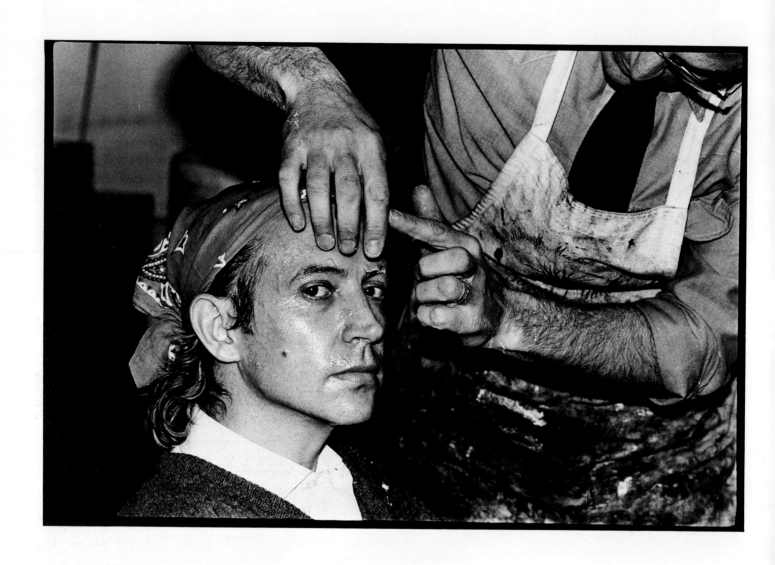

NOTHING CAN EXCEED THE VANITY OF OUR EXISTENCE
BUT THE FOLLY OF OUR PURSUITS □
OLIVER GOLDSMITH: *THE GOOD-NATURED MAN*

IT MAY BE THAT THE STARS OF HEAVEN APPEAR FAIR
AND PURE SIMPLY BECAUSE THEY ARE SO FAR AWAY
FROM US, AND WE KNOW NOTHING OF THEIR PRIVATE
LIFE □ HEINE: *THE ROMANTIC SCHOOL*

SOMEBODY'S BORING ME . . . I THINK IT'S ME □
DYLAN THOMAS

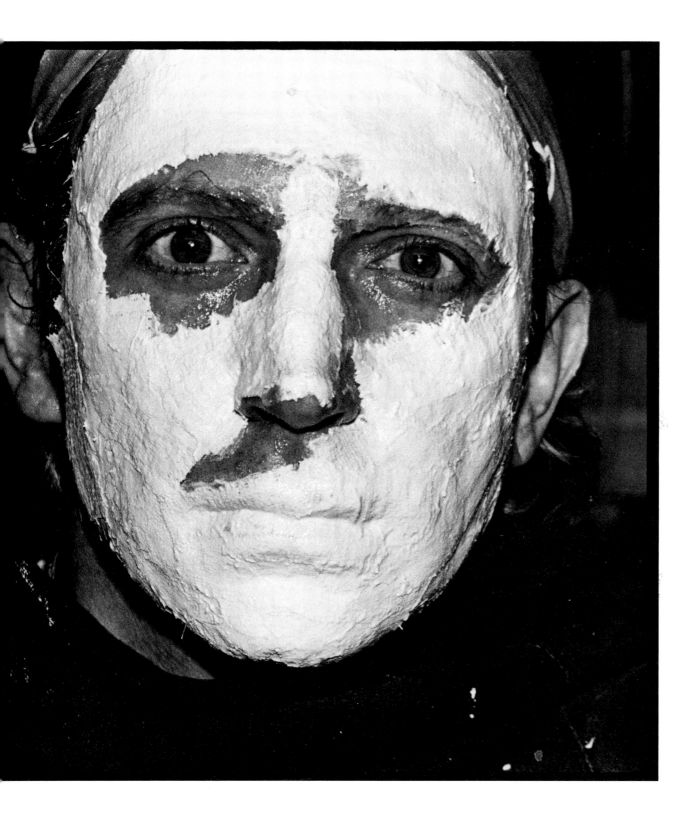

BUT PERHAPS THE UNIVERSE IS SUSPENDED ON THE
TOOTH OF SOME MONSTER □ CHEKHOV:
NOTEBOOKS

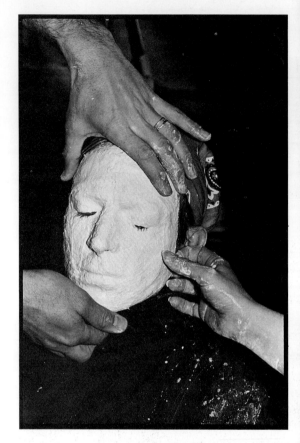

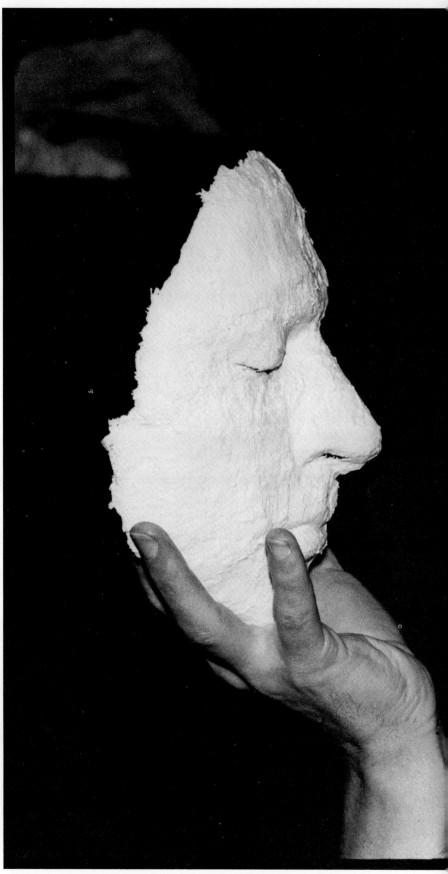

OF ALL LIES, ART IS THE LEAST UNTRUE □
FLAUBERT: *LETTERS*

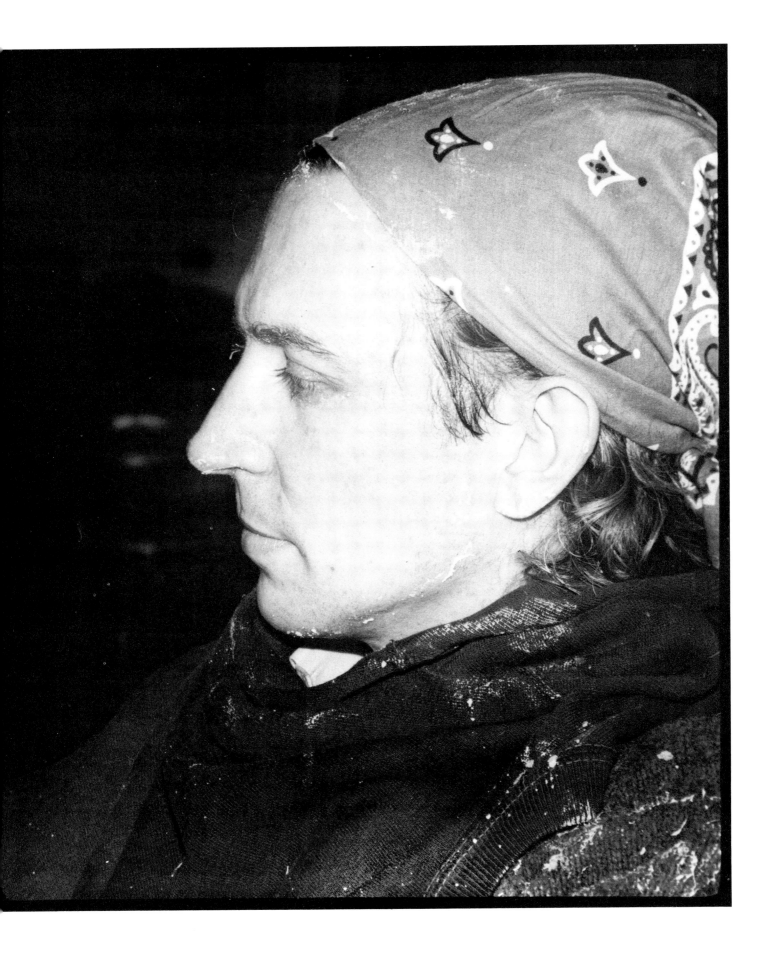

TO THINK IS NOT ENOUGH; YOU MUST THINK OF
SOMETHING □ JULES RENARD: *JOURNAL*

YOU CAN ONLY FIND TRUTH WITH LOGIC IF YOU HAVE
ALREADY FOUND TRUTH WITHOUT IT □ G. K.
CHESTERTON: *THE MAN WHO WAS ORTHODOX*

WHAT IS NOW PROVED WAS ONLY IMAGIN'D □
WILLIAM BLAKE: *THE MARRIAGE OF HEAVEN AND HELL*

GOOD TASTE IS BETTER THAN BAD TASTE, BUT BAD
TASTE IS BETTER THAN NO TASTE AT ALL □
ARNOLD BENNETT

ALL THOUGHTS OF A TURTLE ARE TURTLE □ EMERSON:
JOURNALS

A WISE MAN LAUGHS AT A FOOL; A FOOL DOES THE
SAME BY A WISE MAN, BOTH ARE EQUALLY DIVERTED □
ANONYMOUS: *CHARACTERS AND OBSERVATIONS*

MY FATE CANNOT BE MASTERED: IT CAN ONLY BE
COLLABORATED WITH AND THEREBY, TO SOME EXTENT,
DIRECTED. NOR AM I THE CAPTAIN OF MY SOUL; I AM
ONLY ITS NOISIEST PASSENGER □ ALDOUS HUXLEY:
ADONIS AND THE ALPHABET

IT IS EASIER TO KNOW ONE MAN IN GENERAL THAN TO
UNDERSTAND ONE MAN IN PARTICULAR □
LA ROCHEFOUCAULD: *MAXIMS*

IN EACH OF US THERE IS A LITTLE OF ALL OF US □
LICHTENBERG: *APHORISMS*

WHAT A FINE COMEDY THIS WORLD WOULD BE IF ONE
DID NOT PLAY A PART IN IT! □ DIDEROT: *LETTERS TO
SOPHIE VOLLAND*

DUMONT
BARBER SHOP
When you say,
“take just
a little bit off,”
we take just a
Phone
DANIEL
MARTIN
JOHN
FOWLES

FRIENDSHIP IS A DISINTERESTED COMMERCE BETWEEN
EQUALS; LOVE, AN ABJECT INTERCOURSE BETWEEN
TYRANTS AND SLAVES □ OLIVER GOLDSMITH: *THE
GOOD-NATURED MAN*

WHERE THERE ARE HUMANS YOU'LL FIND FLIES, AND
BUDDHAS □ KOBAYASHI ISSA

GREATNESS IS USUALLY THE RESULT OF NATURAL
EQUILIBRIUM AMONG OPPOSITE QUALITIES □
DIDEROT: *RAMEAU'S NEPHEW*

THE SOLE CAUSE OF MAN'S UNHAPPINESS IS THAT HE
DOES NOT KNOW HOW TO STAY QUIETLY IN HIS
ROOM □ PASCAL: *PENSÉES*

A HIDDEN CONNECTION IS STRONGER THAN AN
OBVIOUS ONE □ HERACLITUS: *FRAGMENTS*

ONLY A BORN ARTIST CAN ENDURE THE LABOUR OF
BECOMING ONE □ COMTESSE DIANE:
MAXIMS DE LA VIE

POPULARITY IS A CRIME FROM THE MOMENT IT IS
SOUGHT: IT IS ONLY A VIRTUE WHERE MEN HAVE IT
WHETHER THEY WILL OR NO □ MARQUESS OF HALIFAX:
MORAL THOUGHTS AND REFLECTIONS

NOT EVERY END IS A GOAL. THE END OF A MELODY IS NOT ITS GOAL;
BUT NONE THE LESS, IF THE MELODY HAD NOT REACHED ITS END IT
WOULD NOT HAVE REACHED ITS GOAL EITHER □ NIETZSCHE: A
PARABLE. *THE WANDERER AND HIS SHADOW*